EXCRETORY SYSTEM

LORRIE KLOSTERMAN

mc Marshall Cavendish
Benchmark

Marshall Cavendish Benchmark
99 White Plains Road
Tarrytown, New York 10591
www.marshallcavendish.us

Editor: Karen Ang
Publisher: Michelle Bisson
Art Director: Anahid Hamparian
Series Design by: Kay Petronio

Library of Congress Cataloging-in-Publication Data

Klosterman, Lorrie.
  Excretory system / by Lorrie Klosterman.
    p. cm. — (The amazing human body)
  Includes bibliographical references and index.
  Summary: "Discusses the parts that make up the human excretory system, what can go wrong, how to treat those illnesses and diseases, and how to stay healthy"—Provided by publisher.
  ISBN 978-0-7614-4037-6
  1. Excretory organs—Juvenile literature. 2. Excretion—Juvenile literature. 3. Feces—Juvenile literature. 4. Urine—Juvenile literature.
  I. Title.
  QP159.K66 2010
  612.4'6—dc22
                      2008037261

Front cover image: A colored X ray of the kidneys
Title page: Kidney cancer cells
Back cover: A microscopic view of glomeruli in the kidneys

 = A microscopic view of the surface of the bladder.

Photo research by Tracey Engel

Front cover photo: David Becker/Getty Images

The photographs in this book are used by permission and through the courtesy of: *Alamy:* Scenics & Science, 10; Phototake, 26; Bartee Photography, Inc./Phototake, p. 36. *Custom Medical Stock Photo:* Educational Images Ltd., 24. *Getty Images:* 3D4Medical.com, 12, 18, 29, 46; Nucleus Medical Art, Inc., 14, 15, 54; Dr. Richard Kessel & Dr. Randy Kardon, 16; Dr. Kessel & Dr. Kardon/Tissues & Organs, 21; Ralph Hutchings, 28; Dr. Dennis Kunkel, 40; David Becker, 47; Tim Boyle, 56; Jeanene Scott, 59. *Photo Researchers, Inc.:* James Cavallini, 4; Volker Steger, 23; SPL, 35 (both); BSIP, 38; John Bavosi, 42, 50; Stephen J. Krasemann, 45; Sam Ogden, 49; AJPhoto / Hôpital Américain, 53; Sheila Terry, 67. *Phototake:* ISM, 20; Craig Zuckerman, 43. *Shutterstock:* Sebastian Kaulitzki, 6; Christina Richards, 7; Antonio Munoz Palomares, 8; Christopher Edwin Nuzzaco, 30; cardiae, 31; Christina Richards, 34; Jim Barber, 41; gresei, 58; Robyn Mackenzie, 60; Elena Elisseeva, 61; mark cinotti, 63; Andi Berger, 64; Thomas M. Perkins, 65; Anetta, 68. *SuperStock:* Image Source, 19, 52. *Visuals Unlimited, Inc.:* Dennis Kunkel Microscopy, Inc., 17, 33.

Printed in Malaysia
123456

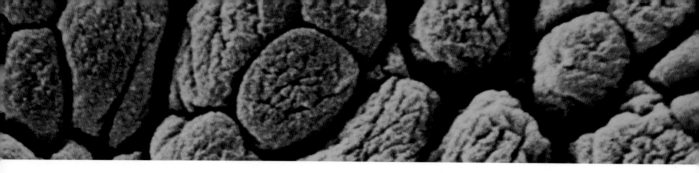

CONTENTS

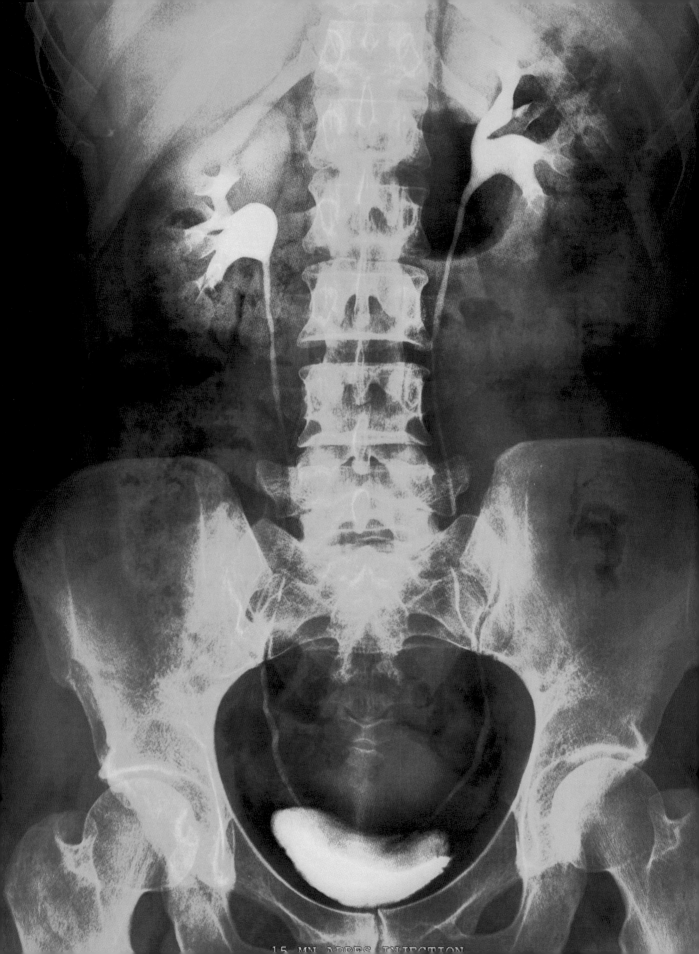

1

What Is the Excretory System?

Every day, when you get hungry or thirsty, your body is telling you that it needs something. Hunger is your body's way of saying that it needs more food to use as fuel. That fuel keeps you alive and active. Thirst is a signal that your body needs more moisture inside. Without the proper amount of moisture, the billions of cells that make up your body cannot survive. In fact, drinking fluids is more important to survival than eating food. Most people could live for many days, or even a few weeks, without food. But nobody can survive for more than a few days without water.

◀ *The excretory system, which is sometimes called the urinary system, is made up of several organs (shown in yellow).*

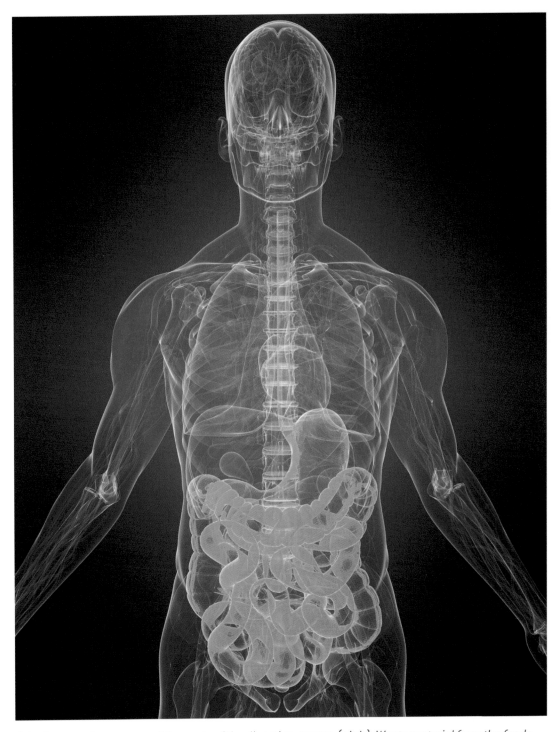

This diagram shows some of the parts of the digestive system (pink). Waste material from the foods you eat and drink are processed and eliminated by your digestive system.

Even though foods and beverages are so important, not every last bit of a meal, or sip of a drink, gets used once it is inside the body. Instead, there is leftover waste. The body's waste materials are familiar to everyone. Things go into our bodies, and things come out.

TWO KINDS OF WASTES

All sorts of words are used to talk about the waste that our bodies make. Solid waste is called feces. To defecate means to get rid of the solid waste. The process of doing that is defecation. Liquid waste from the body is called urine. To urinate means to get rid of liquid waste. The process of doing that is urination.

Urine is a form of liquid waste, and is made up of chemicals and substances that have been removed by organs called kidneys.

WHERE FOOD AND DRINKS GO

Many people believe that solid waste comes from the foods we eat, while liquid waste comes from beverages we drink. That is not true. All things we swallow go into the digestive system. After passing the throat, they go into the stomach, and then into the intestines. Along that journey, foods and beverages are mixed with strong chemicals made by the stomach and intestines. Those chemicals, called digestive enzymes, break up what we have swallowed into pieces that are far too small to see with the naked eye. The pieces then work their way out of the intestines and into nearby blood vessels. The blood within the vessels

Your body processes and uses all of the food and drinks you consume during the course of the day. Some parts of the food and drinks are used to nourish your body, while some is excreted as waste.

carries the bits of food and drink to all parts of the body—wherever the blood goes. That is how a meal fuels the body's needs.

However, there are certain parts of food that our bodies cannot break into pieces very well. That material is called fiber. It gets pushed along the intestines until it reaches the end. There, it collects until the person feels the urge to rid of it by defecating. At that point, the waste is called feces. If a person stops eating for a few days, feces are no longer made.

Liquid waste, or urine, is very different. The internal organs that create urine are not part of the digestive system. Kidneys continue to make urine all the time, even if a person stops eating and drinking.

Feces and urine are made and eliminated, or removed, in two very different ways. Feces are made in the digestive tract. That tract is the long pathway through which foods and beverages travel after you have swallowed them. The beginning of the digestive tract is the mouth. The end is the anus. In between those two are the portions of the tract called the stomach and intestines. In those places, food and beverages are changed into microscopic bits that our bodies can use for energy. But some of what we swallow makes the journey along the digestive tract without being used. It reaches the end and collects as waste. Whenever a person feels the need to defecate, the waste—feces—is released into the toilet.

Urine is made very differently from solid waste. Odd though it may seem, urine is made from blood. Urine is mostly water—as is blood—but urine has several kinds of chemicals that the body does not need. The water and chemicals are taken out of blood by a pair of organs called the kidneys. These remarkable organs are able to cleanse the blood that passes through them, and create a liquid waste—urine. All day and all night the kidneys are at work making urine. Another organ in the body, the bladder, stores the urine for up to several hours. As the bladder gets full, a person feels the need to urinate. Urine flows out of the bladder through a tube that opens to the outside of the body, between a person's legs.

YOUR PERSONAL PLUMBING

Getting rid of feces and urine is just as important as taking in food and water. It is like keeping house. You need to bring in supplies for the household, and you also have to get rid of trash. The body has internal organs that do these jobs. Getting rid of solid waste is one job of the digestive system (the digestive tract, plus other organs that are important in breaking foods into bits). Getting rid of liquid waste is one job of

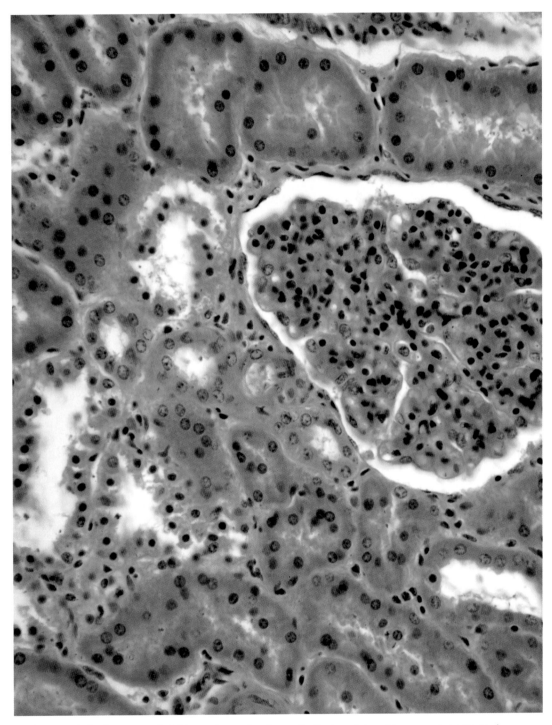

A microscopic look at part of a kidney shows the tiny cells that work hard to remove waste and dangerous substances from your blood.

the urinary system (the kidneys, bladder, and tubes that carry urine).

The urinary system is also called the excretory system. If you have never heard of the excretory system, you are not alone. The word excretory comes from the verb *excrete*. That, in turn, comes from a Latin word meaning "to separate" or "sift out." That is really a good name to describe how urine is made. It is made of materials that are separated out of the blood.

Sometimes people playfully talk about the excretory system as our "plumbing." That is not a bad comparison. The plumbing of a house has pipes that carry water around, just as tubes of the excretory system carry urine around. A house often has a tank that stores water, just as the bladder stores urine. And sometimes a house's pipes get clogged. Blockages in the excretory system happen sometimes, too.

But that is about as far as the plumbing comparison goes. The truth is that the excretory system is far more complex and amazing than it sounds. Besides making urine, the system makes sure that life-giving chemicals are present in the blood in proper amounts. If there is too much or too little of these chemicals, a person will get sick and may die. Without a healthy excretory system the body cannot function.

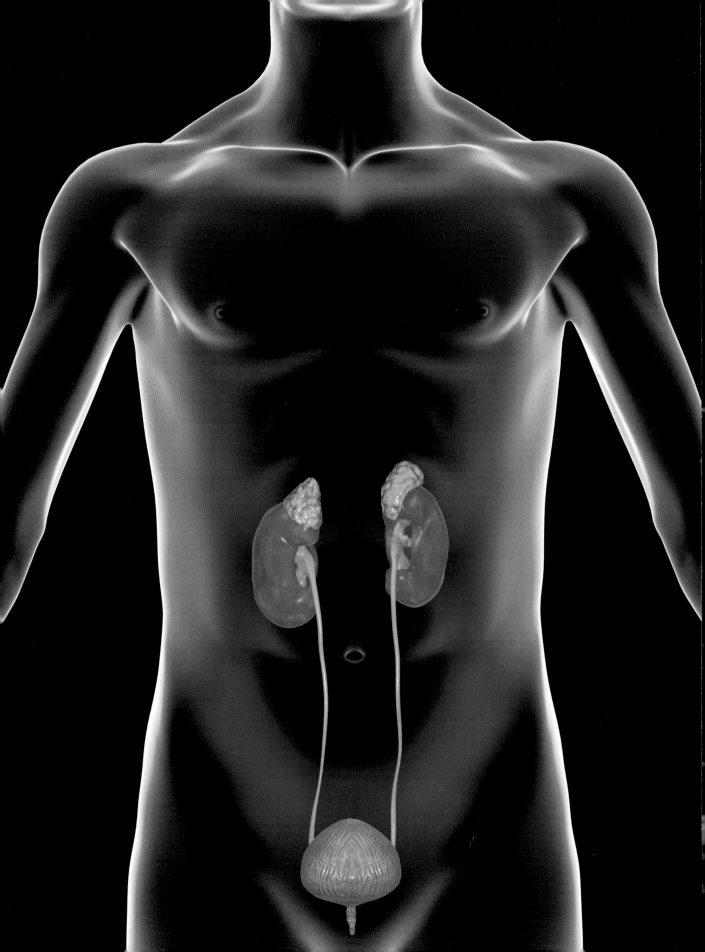

2

The Parts of the Excretory System

The arrangement of the excretory system is quite simple. It has three organs, all located in the abdomen, which is the area between the chest and the hips. Two of these organs, the kidneys, are the main workhorses. They make urine. The third excretory organ is the bladder. It stores the urine that the kidneys make. The ureters are a pair of tubes that bring urine from the kidneys to the bladder. One more tube—the urethra—carries urine from the bladder to an opening between the legs. In females, the urethra ends near the vagina, which is the opening to the reproductive system. In males, the urethra ends at the tip of the penis.

In both men and women, the basic parts of the excretory system—the kidneys, ureters, bladder, and urethra—are the same.

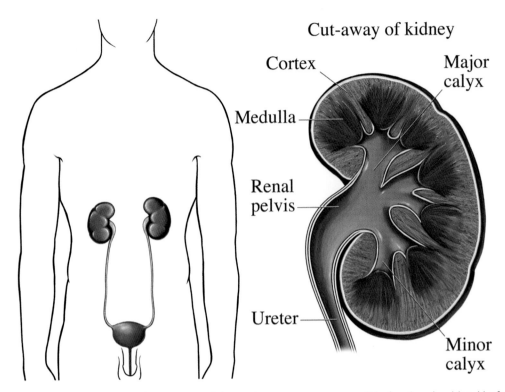

Cut-away of kidney

Cortex

Major calyx

Medulla

Renal pelvis

Ureter

Minor calyx

A cut-away view of a kidney shows some of the main structures responsible for cleaning blood before the urine is drained through the ureter.

Urine is made continually by the kidneys. There is always some flowing out of the kidneys, through the ureters, and into the bladder, where it collects. Every so often, the bladder empties into the urethra, which carries urine outside the body.

That is a very simple summary of what happens in the excretory system. But there is a lot more to making urine than that. A closer look at the kidneys and what they do shows how complex the process actually is.

THE KIDNEYS

If you have ever seen a kidney bean, you have a good idea what a kidney looks like, in miniature. In adults, each kidney is about the size of a large potato, or a large bar of soap. Like a kidney bean, kidneys are reddish-brown and smooth on the surface. Each kidney has a little dent in on one

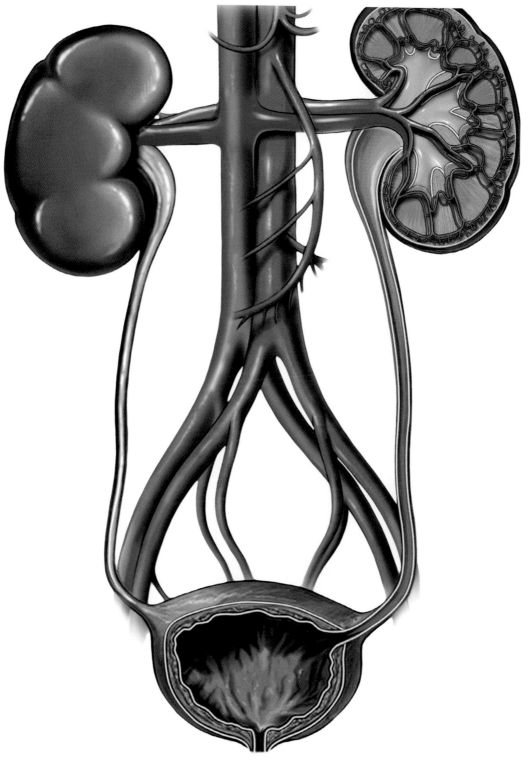

Blood vessels in the kidneys are connected to two of the body's most important blood vessels—the vena cava (blue) and the aorta (red).

side, where a large blood vessel enters and carries blood inside the kidney. Another large vessel carries blood out again. Near these vessels, the ureter leaves the kidneys, carrying urine away.

Each of us has two kidneys, one on the left and one on the right side of the abdomen. (Very rarely, though, some people are born with more than two kidneys, or with only one.) You can get an idea of where your kidneys are by putting your hands on your hips, with your thumbs behind you. Move your hands upward, until you can feel your ribs beneath each hand. The kidneys will be about where your thumbs are, partly protected by your ribs. Each kidney is firmly held in place, pressed against the back of the abdominal cavity, which is the space where many organs are located.

Two Teams of Kidney Cells

The kidney's smooth surface gives no hint about the complex activities going on inside. The inside of a kidney has many different textures and regions. This appearance is due to millions of cells that are grouped together in different ways. Each group of cells does its own task in the urine-making process.

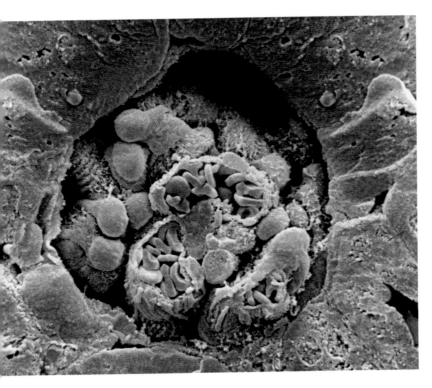

The kidneys are made up of a number of different cells and structures through which blood and waste products travel. The small red objects shown here are blood cells.

This microscopic image has been colored to show the many tiny tubules (blue) inside the kidneys.

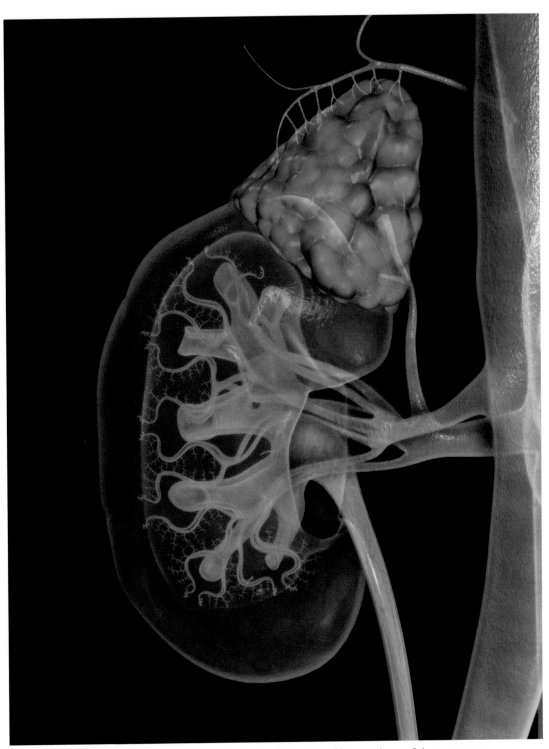

Inside the kidneys are numerous blood vessels that bring blood into and out of those organs.

Many of the cells are grouped into tiny blood vessels. The vessels carry blood all throughout the kidney's interior. The blood that travels in these vessels comes from the large vessel that enters the kidney from outside the organ. Just as the trunk of a tree divides into many smaller branches, that large vessel divides into smaller vessels within the kidney.

Other cells in the kidney are grouped into tiny, hollow tubes called kidney tubules. The tubules are nestled alongside the blood vessels, and are even wrapped around the vessels in some places. The tubules merge with one another in the center of the kidney. There, they connect with the ureter.

Together, the blood vessels and tubules are busy making urine. Fluids and substances are passing out of the blood into the tubules. In the process, the blood gets cleaned up. At the same time, urine is made from the blood's waste materials.

HOW BLOOD BECOMES URINE

If you know something about a car, you may know that it needs oil. Oil flows continually through the engine when the car is running. It allows the engine's parts to move easily against one another. But, over time, oil collects dirt and debris that can hurt the engine. So there is an oil filter, through which the moving oil must pass. As the oil passes through,

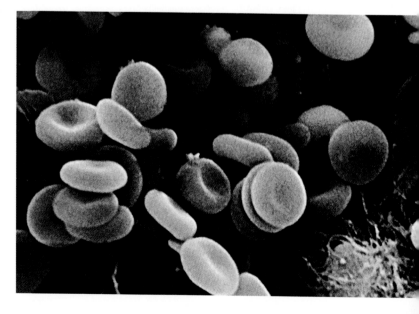

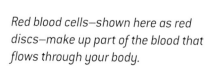

Red blood cells—shown here as red discs—make up part of the blood that flows through your body.

dirt and other material get stuck in the filter. The oil that flows out through the filter is cleaner.

Blood can be compared to oil, and the kidneys to the filter. Waste and debris collect in blood as it flows throughout the body. Inside each kidney, blood vessels form millions of tiny clusters. Each cluster is called a glomerulus (meaning "little ball" in Latin). As blood passes through each glomerulus, some of the blood's water and waste materials leak out.

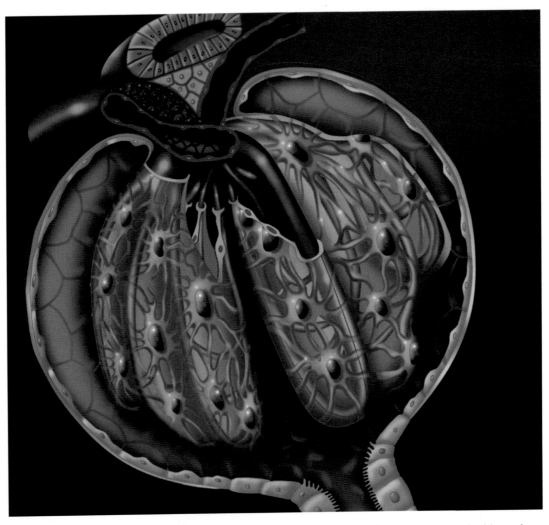

An illustrated cross-section of a glomerulus shows the tiny blood vessels and structures inside each cluster.

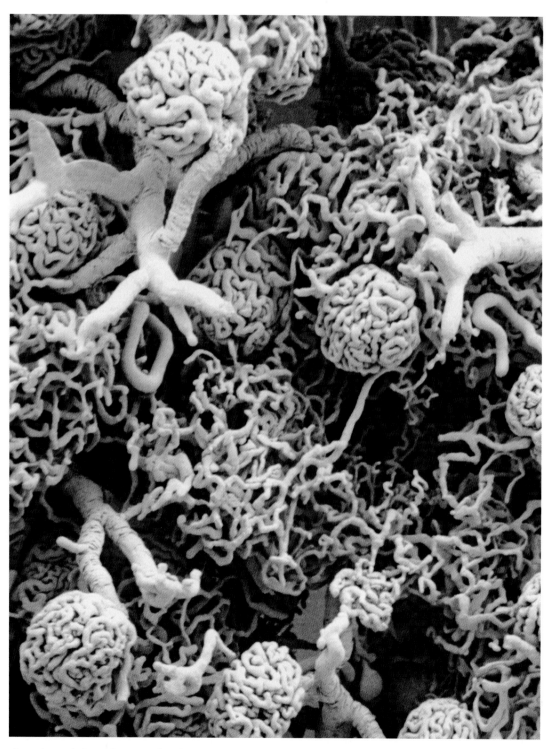

An enlarged view of a part of a kidney shows the millions of glomeruli that filter out waste.

The cleaner blood then flows on, leaving the glomerulus, and travels back out of the kidney.

The waste remains in the kidney—but not for long. The fluid and waste that leaked out of the blood collects in tiny tubules nestled all through the kidney. The fluid, which is now urine, flows into the ureter and leaves the kidney. Its next stop is the bladder, to eventually be eliminated from the body.

WHEN IT IS TIME TO "GO"

The kidneys make urine all the time. So why do we only need to urinate every few hours? It is because we have a storage vessel for urine—the bladder. The bladder holds urine that comes from the kidneys. As it fills, the bladder stretches, like a balloon slowly filling with air. It cannot stretch forever, though. At some point, the body has to empty the bladder.

Thanks to nerves that connect the bladder with the brain, we get warnings ahead of time. Those nerves notice when the bladder is getting stretched. They send signals to the brain. When those signals reach the brain, we become aware of the need to urinate.

What keeps the bladder from emptying before we are ready? A special structure keeps urine from leaving the body before you are ready to release it. That structure is called a sphincter. It is made of muscle, and it surrounds the urethra like a ring, near the point where the urethra and bladder meet. Because the sphincter is made of muscle, it can both stretch and contract, or tighten. Usually, it is contracted. That keeps urine in. To let it out, the sphincter needs to relax. Signals from the brain let the muscle relax. That allows urine to flow into the urethra and out of the body.

To use the balloon comparison, imagine a balloon filled with air, and your fingers holding the balloon closed. Your fingers are like the sphincter.

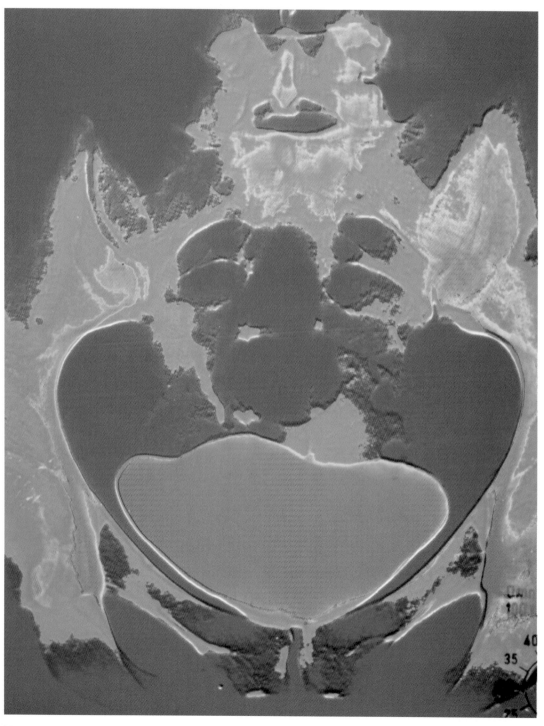

The bladder expands as urine collects inside. This colored X ray shows a bladder partially filled with urine (orange).

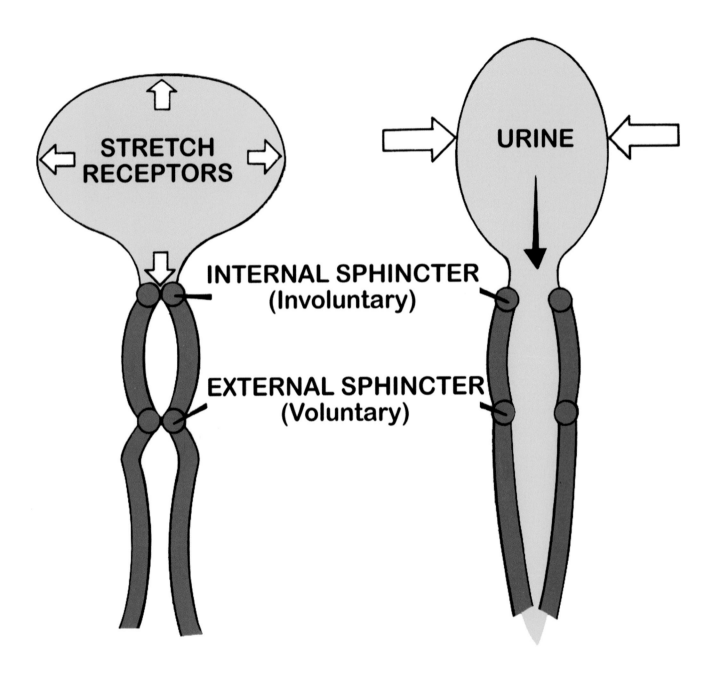

STRETCH RECEPTORS

URINE

INTERNAL SPHINCTER
(Involuntary)

EXTERNAL SPHINCTER
(Voluntary)

Stretch receptors inside the bladder (left) alert the body that urine needs to be released. As a result, the body relaxes the sphincters to excrete the urine (right). Control of the internal sphincter is involuntary, which means you cannot control when it tightens or relaxes. You can, however, control the external sphincter.

As long as you hold them tight, the air will not come out. But as soon as you loosen your grip, air flows out.

Each of us learns, as a toddler, to control the urge to urinate until we get to a bathroom. But we are not born with the ability. That is why babies and toddlers need diapers. Their bladders empty many times a day without the child's control. It takes about three to four years for a youngster to master the ability to hold urine until the appropriate time. The body must be mature enough. The urinary system, the nervous system, and the brain all must develop to a point where they can work together to control emptying the bladder.

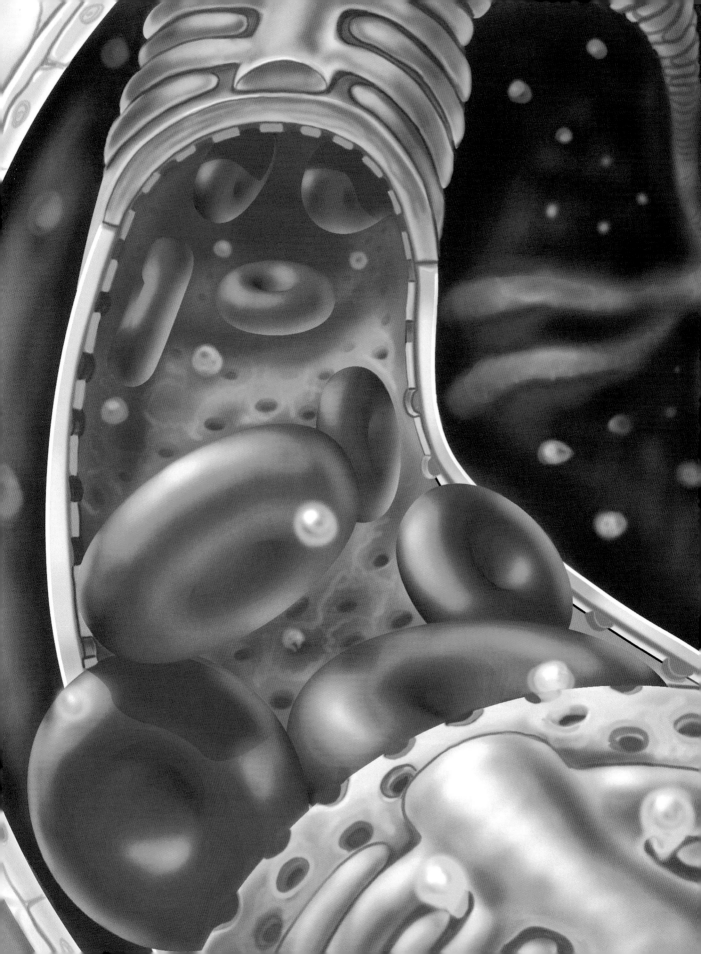

3

How the Excretory System Works

The most obvious job of the excretory system is making urine. The kidneys do this all day long, and also during the night while we sleep, though more slowly. But kidneys do several other tasks at the same time they make urine. Your body strives to keep itself in a healthy internal balance. That balance is called homeostasis, and kidneys play an important role in this.

One of the kidneys' tasks is controlling, or regulating, the amount of water in the body. Kidneys make sure there is not too much water, and not too little. For instance, if somebody has quickly gulped down a large bottle of water, the body will have more liquid than it can use. So the kidneys will put the extra liquid into urine.

◀ *This illustration shows red blood cells passing through the tiny tubes inside a glomerulus.*

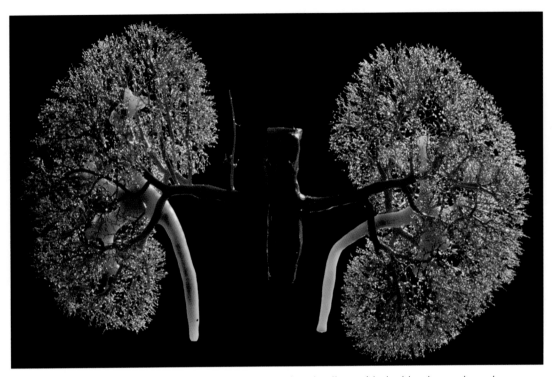

In this model of the human kidneys, the ureters are colored yellow, with the blood vessels and glomeruli shown in red and pink.

Kidneys also control the amounts of other essential substances in the body. For example, we all need salt (sodium) in our bodies, but in the right amount. If somebody has eaten a meal that has a lot of salt in it, the kidneys can get rid of the excess salt in urine.

Kidneys also clean the blood of cellular waste—the worn out bits of molecules that all cells make during their normal activities. Kidneys rid the body of foreign substances, too. Those are things that do not belong in us at all, such as poisons and manmade chemicals.

KEEPING YOU PERFECTLY MOIST

In a way, the insides of our bodies might be compared to soup. It is mostly water, but has many different kinds of nutrients and other substances

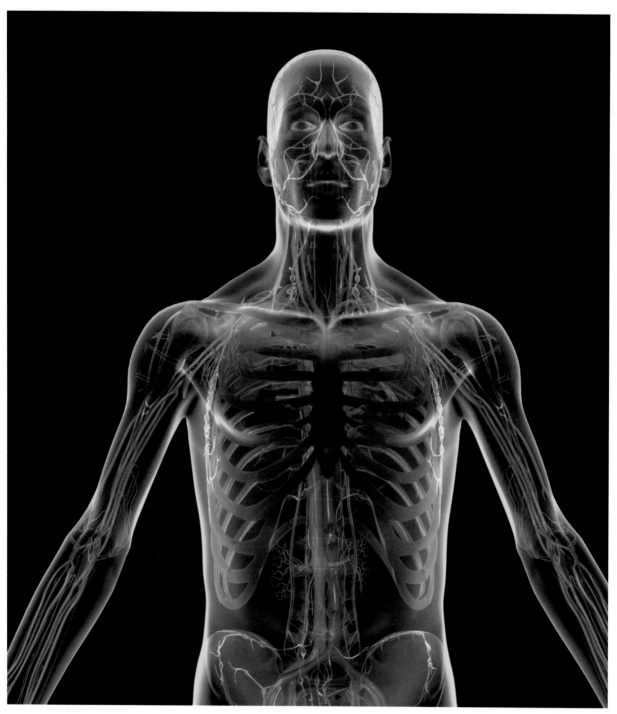

Blood is transported through many different vessels throughout the body. It removes waste from the different organs and brings oxygen, nutrients, and other helpful substances.

Your body is mostly made up of water, and needs it for important processes. In order to stay healthy, you must provide your body with enough water.

floating in it. Our cells live in this "soup." To function well, all living cells need to be in a moist environment that has the right amounts of water and other substances.

Too much water can actually be quite dangerous. It makes our internal environment too diluted, or watered down. The problem with this is that cells are then surrounded by too much water, and not enough of the materials they need to stay alive. Cells need the right amount of nutrients around them to be healthy. Imagine, by comparison, that you are making soup that you usually enjoy, but by mistake you add far too much water. The soup will be a thin broth that is not as satisfying or nutritious as usual.

On the other hand, kidneys also make sure the body's interior does not get too dry. Cells cannot survive this condition, which is called dehydration.

They need a moist, fluid environment. Using the soup comparison, a dehydrated body is like a soup that is a concentrated thick paste. The soup would be too strong, and it would not go down very easily.

KEEPING YOU PERFECTLY SALTY

Kidneys control the amounts of electrolytes in the body. Electrolytes are chemicals that are essential for a variety of life-supporting activities. Electrolytes include sodium, potassium, chloride, calcium, magnesium, phosphates, and many others. Sodium is the most plentiful of these, and it is sometimes referred to as salt. (Table salt—called sodium chloride—is made up of sodium.)

Salt is essential for many body processes, but too much or too little can cause problems. Much of the salt in your body comes from the salt in your food and drinks.

Like water, electrolytes in the body need to be present in the right amounts. If any of these electrolytes begins to accumulate, the kidneys allow the excess to leave the body in urine. An example of an electrolyte is sodium. It is very plentiful in foods and beverages, so you are always consuming more than your body needs. Kidneys allow enough sodium to leave the body, so that the amount remains within a normal range.

Kidneys also are able to prevent electrolytes from being lost in urine, if the body needs more of them. Potassium is an example of an electrolyte the body needs, but which sometimes becomes too scarce. (This is often because potassium is not as abundant in our foods as sodium.) Kidneys are very good at making sure potassium does not end up in urine when the body needs it.

CLEANSING BLOOD

Urine is called waste because it has things in it the body does not need. Water and electrolytes, though necessary for life, are treated as waste when there is too much of them. But there are also true waste materials in urine—substances the body has no use for. In fact, they can poison cells and make a person sick if they accumulate in the bloodstream. The kidneys get these poisons out of blood and dispose of them in urine.

What kinds of poisons can be in the bloodstream? Some are manmade chemicals that have been swallowed, inhaled, or absorbed through the skin. Poisons work their way into the bloodstream, and can harm cells they reach. Examples are chemical cleaners, pesticides (poisons used to kill insects), and toxic metals. Kidneys take these out as best they can. Kidneys are not able to remove all poisons from the body. Sometimes some substances collect inside of certain types of body cells, such as fat cells, and are no longer traveling in the bloodstream where the kidneys can remove them.

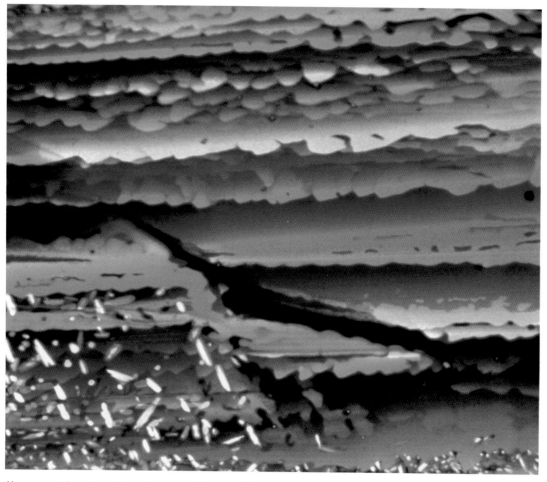

Urea crystals, shown here in a special type of photograph, are a type of nitrogenous waste that is filtered through the kidneys and excreted in urine.

Sometimes the toxic substance is something a person has taken intentionally, but in excess. Too many alcoholic beverages or too much medication are examples. In small amounts, these are usually safe. But in larger amounts they can harm cells before the kidneys have time to get rid of the excess.

The most common toxins the body needs to get rid of are made by the body itself. They are waste molecules that cells make as part of their everyday activities. The waste molecules collect outside of the cells. They drift into the bloodstream and are carried away. The waste is removed when it goes through the kidneys. The most toxic kinds of cellular waste have nitrogen in them, and the body works hard to remove these wastes. The most abundant of these nitrogenous wastes is urea. Urea and other nitrogenous wastes that are excreted through urine change into ammonia if urine is exposed to air for a while. Ammonia is a pungent-smelling gas. This is why babies' diapers often smell like ammonia.

KEEPING YOU IN ACID-BASE BALANCE

Kidneys also make sure our interiors do not become too acidic or basic. Acidic means having an abundance of acids. Acids are chemicals that can damage living cells. Basic (also called alkaline) means having an abundance of bases. Bases also can damage living cells. Acids and bases are plentiful in the natural world. They exist in our foods and in our bodies all the time. For instance, citrus fruits, tomatoes, and pickled foods are acidic, and many cellular activities create acids as waste products. Milk and many vegetables are basic, and a few cellular activities create bases.

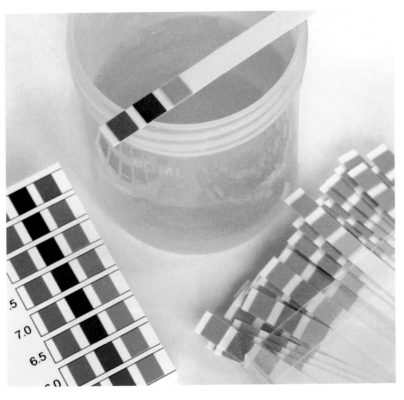

Chemical test strips can test the acidity of urine. This is called testing its pH.

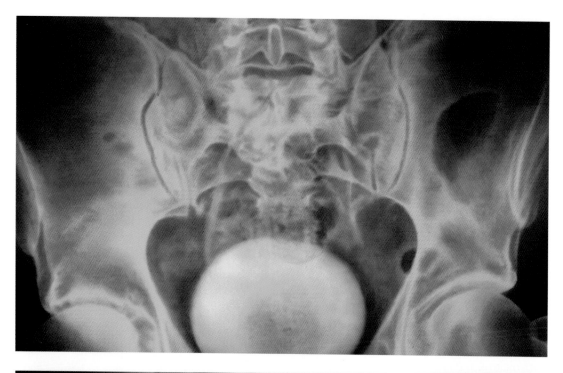

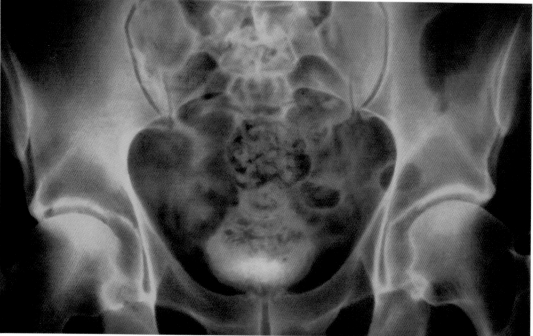

When the bladder is full (top), a healthy excretory system will empty it (bottom) of the urine. Urine that stays in the body too long can cause problems like infections or other illnesses.

HEALTH CHECK-UP IN A CUP

When you visit the doctor, you might be asked to give a urine sample. A urine sample is a simple way for a doctor to get a lot of information about what is going on inside your body. The urine is usually sent to a laboratory where it is analyzed. Laboratory technicians measure all kinds of substances in urine. Some of the measurements are done simply by dipping special strips of paper into the urine. The paper will turn different colors if certain substances are present. One thing the strips show is sugar. A urine sample from a healthy person should not have any sugar in it. But if the paper strip turns color, sugar is there. That is a sign that the kidneys are not working properly, or that there is too much sugar in the bloodstream. Laboratory

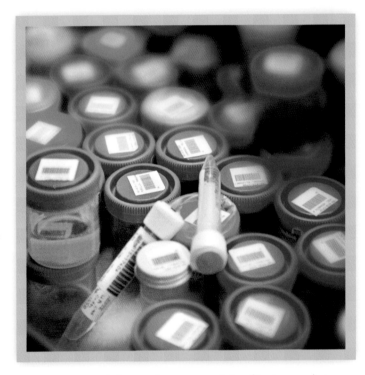

Laboratories run a variety of tests on urine samples. The kind of test performed depends on why the urine is being tested.

technicians also look for cells and blood in urine. They do this by looking at tiny drops of urine with a microscope. Cells and blood are signs of injury or infection somewhere in the urinary system.

In order to function properly, our cells must live in a nearly neutral environment—just a bit on the basic side, actually. Neutral means that the amount of acids and bases are just about equal, and they cancel each other out. With all the acids and bases that come into the body as foods, and the ones that are made through the body's everyday activities, there must be a way to make sure the body's fluids stay neutral. The excretory system does a big part of that work. Kidneys excrete extra acid in urine. (Sometimes they dispose of extra bases, but much less often.) Just how they do this is an impressively complex process. The final outcome, though, is that fluids are not out of balance for long, thanks to the acid-base balancing skills of kidneys.

Kidneys and the other parts of the excretory system play a vital role in maintaining the body's homeostasis. When the excretory system is affected by diseases or injury, the body cannot function properly. Damage to the excretory system may become a life-threatening matter.

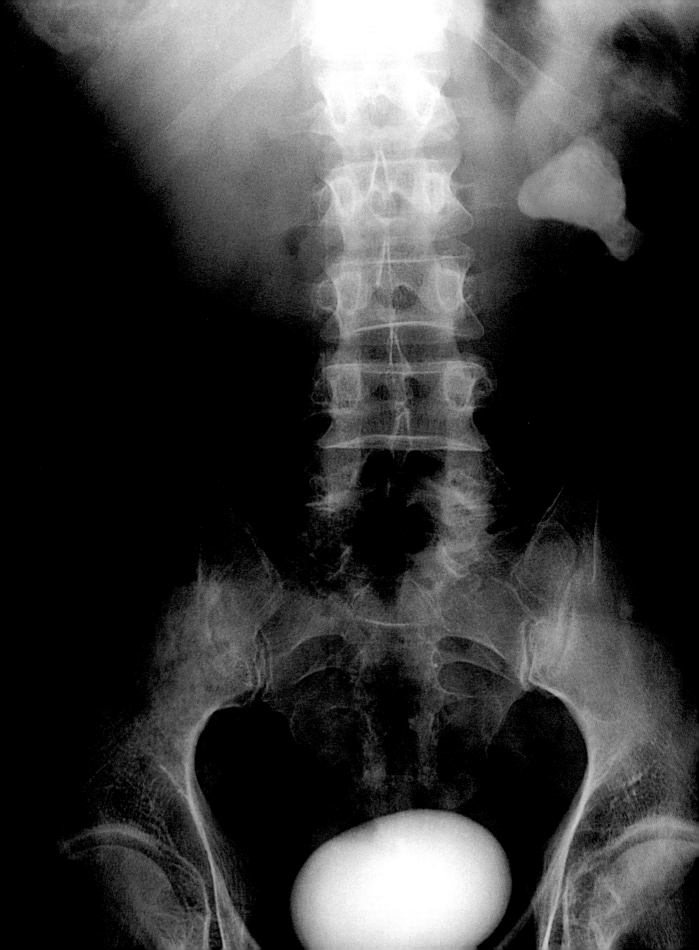

4

Problems with the Excretory System

Most of us hardly notice the excretory system at work. Sure, we use the toilet a few times a day. But we never think about the many activities going on inside—until something goes wrong. The excretory system can get infected, injured, or diseased. The problem might be rather simple, such as a short-lived infection that makes urinating painful for a few days. But very serious conditions can arise, too, and may even be life threatening.

◄ *Kidney stones are one of the most common problems with the excretory system. This X ray reveals a large kidney stone (yellow) stuck in this person's left kidney.*

URINARY TRACT INFECTIONS

Just like other parts of the body, the excretory system can become infected. That means that pathogens—disease-causing bacteria, viruses, or parasites—have settled in among healthy cells and are harming them. Infections of the excretory system are known as urinary tract infections, or UTIs. Bacteria are usually to blame. Bacteria are plentiful on the skin, and usually are harmless there. But if they work their way into the urethra, they can infect it. Even worse, because the urethra is a tube, it acts like a tunnel along which bacteria can travel to the bladder. Bladder infections are fairly common, especially in females, because their urethra is shorter than that of males.

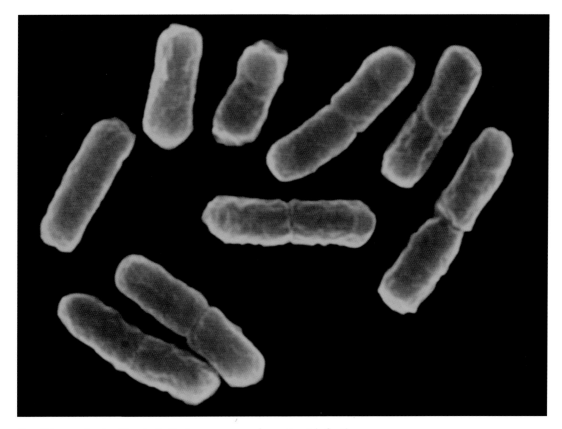

E. coli is one form of bacteria that can cause urinary tract infections.

An infected urethra or bladder usually makes urinating painful. A person with a UTI might experience pain or burning while urinating; feeling the urge to urinate more often than usual; urinating only small quantities at a time; urine that is cloudy, not clear; urine that is tinged with red, which is a sign of blood; pain or pressure in the lower part of the abdomen or back; and fever. If you notice any of these things, a simple visit to the doctor, where you will leave a urine sample, can reveal whether a UTI is the culprit. The urine sample, when studied by laboratory technicians, may show signs of infection. Those signs are bacteria, bits of cells, proteins, or blood in the urine. If there is an infection, treatment is simple—usually taking antibiotic (bacteria-killing) medication for a few weeks, and drinking a lot of fluids to help wash bacteria out of the system.

KIDNEY INFECTIONS

Sometimes bacteria that have settled into the bladder can spread to the kidneys by way

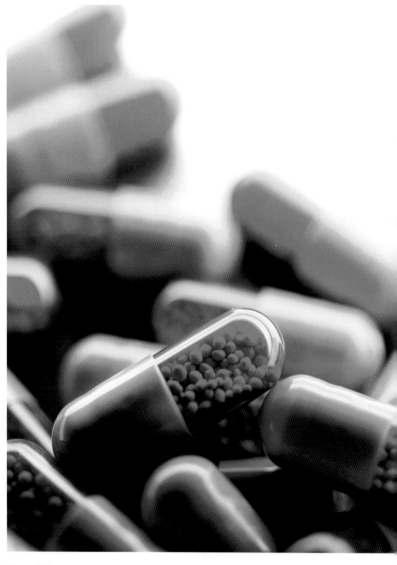

Most UTIs can be treated with medications like antibiotics.

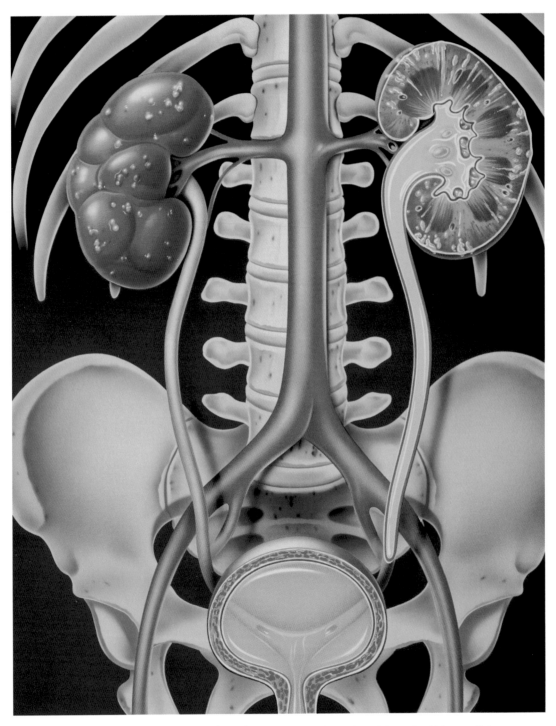

When ureters do not function correctly (right) urine may be forced back into the kidneys. This can cause painful kidney infections, shown here as yellow streaks in inside the kidney.

of the ureters. Usually the flow of urine going down the ureters prevents this. Still, bacteria occasionally work their way up into one or both kidneys. Bacteria can also enter the kidneys through the bloodstream. An infected kidney is a serious matter. Bacteria release chemicals that injure cells. Fluid collects in the infected kidney, too, and the organ gets swollen. A swollen kidney cannot make urine well, and it causes a lot of pain. A kidney infection can become so bad that the organ is damaged beyond repair.

Fortunately, there are noticeable symptoms of a kidney infection. These include pain in the abdomen or back, a fever, and pain while urinating.

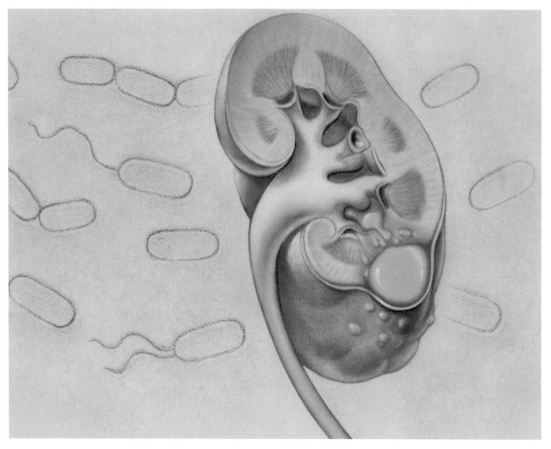

Infections can cause an abscess—or an inflamed area, shown here as a yellow mass—in the kidney. With proper treatment, abscesses usually go away on their own, but very large ones may need to be opened up and drained by a doctor.

LIQUID CLUES TO THE INNER YOU

A urine test is a fast, simple way to look for signs of some internal problems. That is why many doctors ask for a urine sample during a regular checkup. Urine is made mostly of water, and normally has in it a collection of waste materials, such as urea, uric acid, electrolytes, urochrome (old hemoglobin), and worn out bits of hormones and vitamins. But certain things that show up in a urine test are not normal. Here are some of them, and what they may mean.

Substance	Possible Problem
glucose (the body's most abundant sugar)	too much sugar in the diet; diabetes
proteins	excessive exercise or dieting; kidney infection or disease; high blood pressure; heart damage
red blood cells or hemoglobin (from inside red blood cells)	urinary tract infection or injury; kidney stones; kidney or bladder cancer; illnesses that kill red blood cells
white blood cells	urinary tract infection
drugs or similar molecules	recent drug use (within several hours or days)
bacteria	bacterial infection somewhere in the urinary system

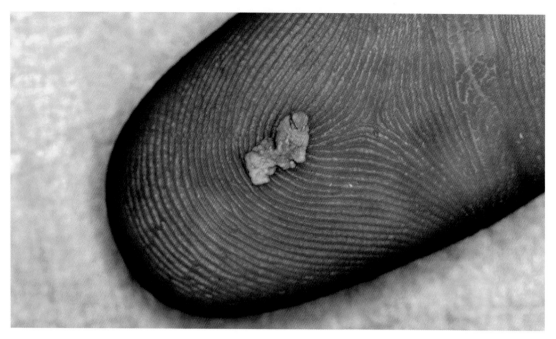

Kidney stones can range in size, and some may be as small as the one shown here on a fingertip. However, even a small kidney stone can cause pain.

Someone with these symptoms should see a doctor right away. At the doctor's office, testing the person's urine will show whether the problem is truly kidney infection. The presence of blood, bacteria, immune cells, or protein all point to infection. A doctor can prescribe antibiotics, which usually clears the infection in a few days or weeks.

KIDNEY STONES

A health problem called kidney stones is rarely fatal, but it can be extremely painful. Kidney stones are hard objects that form in the kidneys when calcium, magnesium, or other materials in urine clump together. The stones made by these materials have no way out of the kidney except by traveling down the ureter. Many stones are small, and can make that journey with ease. They then are expelled from the body during urination. This is often called passing a stone.

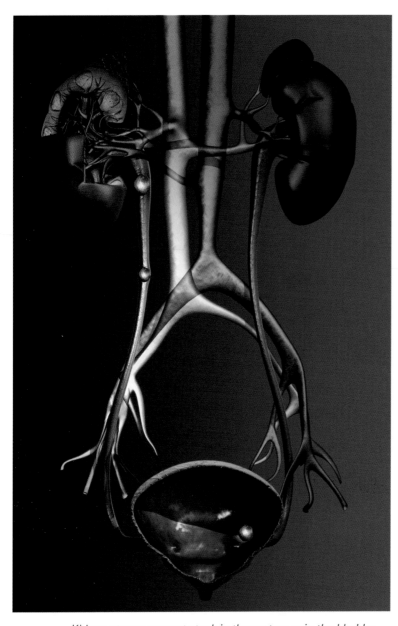

Kidney stones can get stuck in the ureters or in the bladder. Usually, the stones in the bladder will be passed through urination.

However, some stones are large enough that they cause a great deal of pain as they move around in the bladder or travel along the ureter. Sometimes they get stuck in the ureter.

When this happens, the stones prevent the flow of urine along the ureter. Urine then collects behind the stone, causing the kidney to swell. Pressure in the kidney from the accumulating urine can be very painful.

In many cases, a doctor can remove some kidney stones through surgery. Another way of treating kidney stones, which does not require surgery, is ultrasound. This procedure uses sound waves—too low for human ears to detect— that cause vibrations when they travel through the body. A medical technician places a device that emits ultrasound waves on the skin near the kidney. The waves can break the stone into tiny pieces, which then easily move along the ureter and flow out of the body through urine.

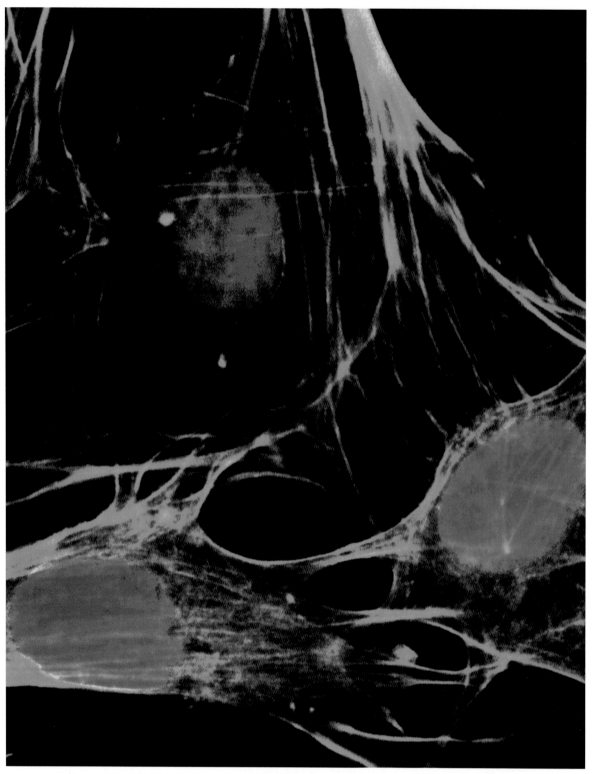

These cells (red and green) are a type of cancer that affects the kidneys.

CANCER

The kidneys and bladder can develop cancer. Cancer occurs when some of the body's cells become changed, or mutated, so that they no longer behave as they should. Instead, these mutated cells make more and more copies of themselves, and begin to create a mass called a malignant tumor. This becomes a dangerous situation when the tumor becomes large enough to crowd out normal cells, and damage organs. (Benign tumors are not as dangerous as malignant ones.)

Fortunately, kidney cancer usually only develops in one kidney. That kidney can be removed, taking the tumor with it, and the remaining kidney will continue to work just fine. Sometimes, though, cancer cells have also spread elsewhere, to vital organs like the lungs, liver, or brain. In those cases, a person's chances of survival are smaller. About 50,000 people in the United States get kidney cancer each year. Almost all of them are over the age of 45. Unfortunately, about a fourth of them eventually die from it.

About 60,000 people in the United States get bladder cancer each year. A fourth of these people eventually die from bladder cancer. If the cancer is found when the tumor is small, chemicals or medication can be put directly into the bladder to help kill the cancer cells. One such medication is actually a kind of bacteria called BCG. When BCG is put in the bladder, the patient's immune system goes to work killing the BCG. In the process, the immune system also destroys the cancer cells.

For bladder cancer that is more advanced, some or all of the bladder may need to be surgically removed. To replace it, doctors may create a similar shaped organ and connect it to the ureters and urethra. That surgery is still being perfected, though. It is more common for a patient to have a tube put in to drain urine outside the body. The tube usually exits the body through a small hole near the belly button. A bag is attached to the tube, and can be emptied as it fills.

AN ARTIFICIAL BLADDER MAKES HISTORY

Doctors and medical researchers are always looking for new ways to help their patients. One of the biggest challenges is helping patients who have an organ that is too injured or diseased to ever work properly again. When that is the case, one solution is organ transplantation. In that process, doctors remove a healthy organ from a donor and implant it into the patient. That often works well. But healthy organs are in short supply. So researchers are trying to create artificial organs—ones that are made entirely in the laboratory.

This is no easy task. Recently, though, a group of researchers has been able to make an artificial bladder. It is the first organ made of living cells rather than being made of plastics, metals, or other nonliving materials. The researchers used human cells from samples of a young girl's own, damaged bladder. They "grew" more of the cells in nutrient-rich liquids. Over a few weeks, the researchers were able to grow different kinds of cells around a small sphere-like structure imitating the way a human bladder is constructed. They then transplanted this artificial bladder into the girl. The bladder is not a perfect copy of a real bladder, but it worked quite well, and has helped the girl to lead a much more normal life.

A scientist holds an artificial bladder that was grown from human bladder cells.

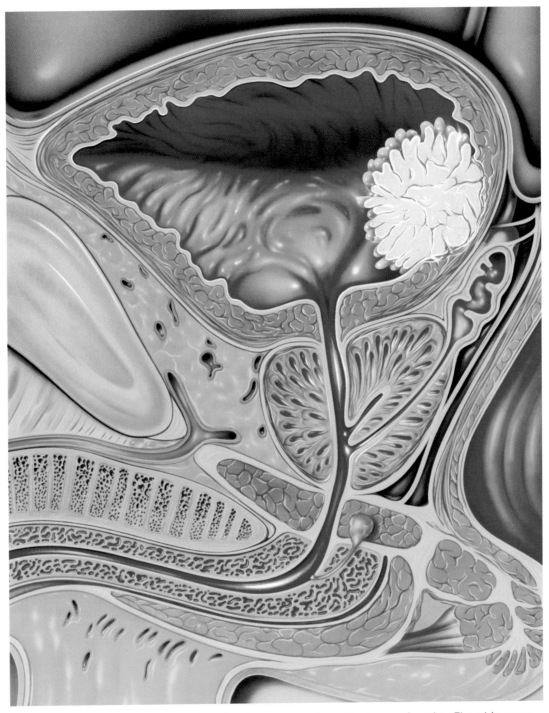

When many cancer cells group together, they form tumors that affect organ function. The white structure (upper right) is a cancerous tumor that is attached to the wall of the bladder.

Why does one person get cancer and another not? There is no clear answer, but scientists have found that there are some risk factors, which make it more likely for a person to develop kidney or bladder cancer. (Many of these risk factors apply to other types of cancers, too). The risk factors include smoking, obesity (being very overweight), having high blood pressure, being exposed to toxic chemicals and to certain medications, and radiation. The chances of getting cancer also may be inherited from a parent. But, if a parent developed kidney or bladder cancer that does not make it certain their children will.

KIDNEY FAILURE

Sometimes a kidney becomes so damaged that it fails. Kidney failure means that a kidney is not able to carry out some (or many) of its life-sustaining tasks. It is possible for one kidney to fail, while the other remains healthy. A car crash or other accidental injury might damage on kidney, but not the other. In these cases, doctors will remove the damaged one. It is quite possible to live a normal life with one healthy kidney.

Kidney failure can be temporary, such as during a serious kidney infection. The kidney may start working fine again once the infection goes away. But infections can sometimes be so damaging that kidney cells are killed and replaced by scar tissue. Scar tissue cannot do what kidney cells can. So the kidney may not work as well as it once did.

Another cause of kidney failure is a disease that harms the glomeruli—the clusters of blood vessels that leak the fluids that make up urine. Medical researchers are still trying to understand exactly what happens in this kind of disease. It seems that the body's own immune cells attack the glomeruli. They might do that if pathogens have entered the bloodstream and then get trapped in the glomeruli. Immune cells then do their jobs and kill the invading pathogens and accidentally harm the glomeruli, too.

Kidneys can also fail when the vessels bringing in blood get blocked. Kidneys cannot do any of their jobs without enough blood. The most common reason vessels get blocked is plaque. Plaque is made of fat, cholesterol, cells, and other materials. It sticks to the inside of blood vessels, making it hard for blood to get by. Kidney failure because of plaque is more common in middle-aged or older people, in obese people, and in people with diabetes.

High blood pressure damages kidneys, too. This condition occurs when blood exerts a lot of pressure against blood vessels as it travels through them. That makes it more likely that smaller, fragile blood vessels will burst. High blood pressure is common in people with diabetes, so the two problems together put kidneys at risk of injury.

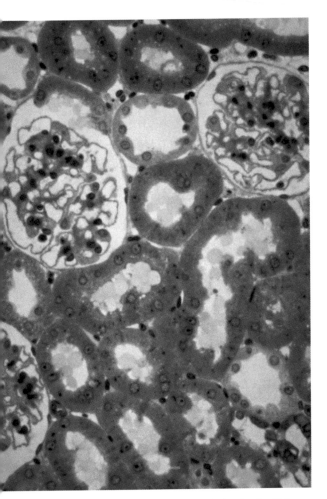

If the glomeruli and tubules in the kidneys are damaged, they cannot properly filter out waste, and infections may set in.

Treating Kidney Failure

If kidneys are too diseased to function, toxins rapidly build up in the bloodstream. When the kidneys fail, doctors must do one of two things—the patient must undergo dialysis or have a kidney transplant.

Dialysis is a process done in a doctor's office or hospital a few times a week. Dialysis treatment mimics the kidneys' job of cleansing the blood. The patient is connected by tubing to a machine that acts as a filter. The tube carries blood

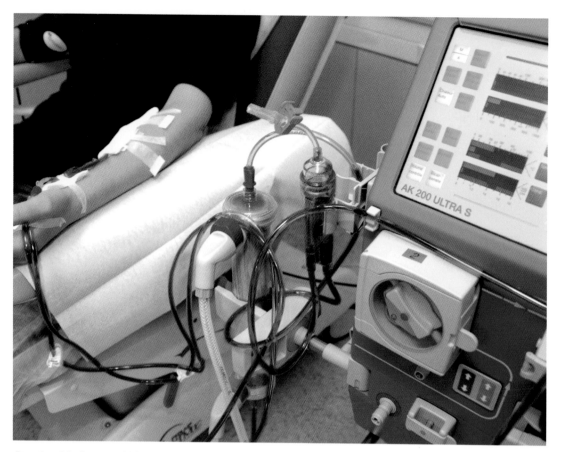

People with damaged kidneys need to undergo dialysis treatments until their body is once again able to properly filter wastes from their blood.

outside the person's body, through the machine—where toxins are filtered out—and then back into the patient. The process takes several hours each time. Some people get a home-dialysis machine and take training so they can do the dialysis treatments at home with the help of a nurse or family member. Dialysis can be used until the kidneys recover or until a new kidney is transplanted. If the kidney does not recover and a transplant is not performed, dialysis may be done for the rest of the patient's life.

Transplanting a kidney means surgically putting a kidney from another person, called a donor, into the patient. A family member sometimes offers to donate a kidney. Often, the patient must wait until a kidney is available from someone who has died and donated their organs. But not just any kidney will do. It must be a good match. Every person has a unique set of proteins in their organs, and for a transplant to work, the proteins of the

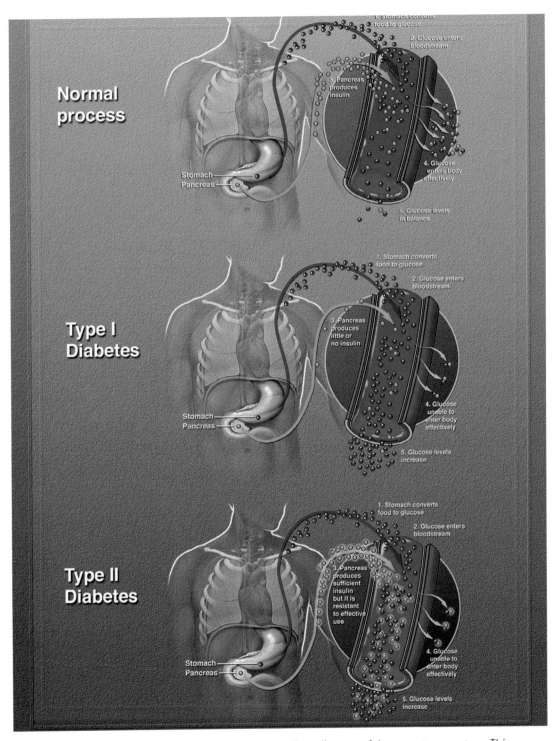

Though it can cause kidney failure, diabetes is not really a disease of the excretory system. This illustration shows the two different types of diabetes, and how the body is supposed to manage insulin (a necessary protein) and blood sugar.

donor and the patient must be very similar. That is why a family member makes a good donor: they share many traits, including proteins.

DIABETES AND KIDNEYS

The illness called diabetes mellitus (diabetes for short) is not really a disease of the excretory system, but the kidneys are involved. Diabetes is a condition in which the body cannot properly control how much sugar is in the bloodstream. Although everybody must have a bit of sugar in the blood—because it fuels cells' activities—too much sugar is dangerous. The excess collects inside blood vessels, and it also seems to have something to do with plaque formation. People with diabetes have poor blood circulation because of the clogged and damaged vessels.

How are kidneys involved in diabetes? The kidneys' blood vessels can get damaged and clogged with plaque. Then the kidney cells do not get enough blood, and they gradually die off. The dead parts of a kidney are replaced by scar tissue. Scar tissue is tough and strong, but it can never turn back into kidney cells. So the kidney cannot make its usual amount of urine. At the same time, it cannot clean blood well, and waste materials build up. Because waste materials are toxic, other parts of the body, like the brain, can be poisoned.

Diabetes is the number one cause of kidney failure in adults. Each year in the United States, tens of thousands of people with diabetes experience kidney failure. And there are not many signs that their kidneys are getting damaged until it is too late. Some good news, though, is that people who have diabetes can make changes that will protect their kidneys. Doctors have discovered that a low-fat diet with a lot of nutritious vegetables and lean meats—plus a moderate amount of exercise—helps keep blood vessels healthy and can even remove plaque. So people who make these kinds of lifestyle changes may be saving their kidneys as well as their lives.

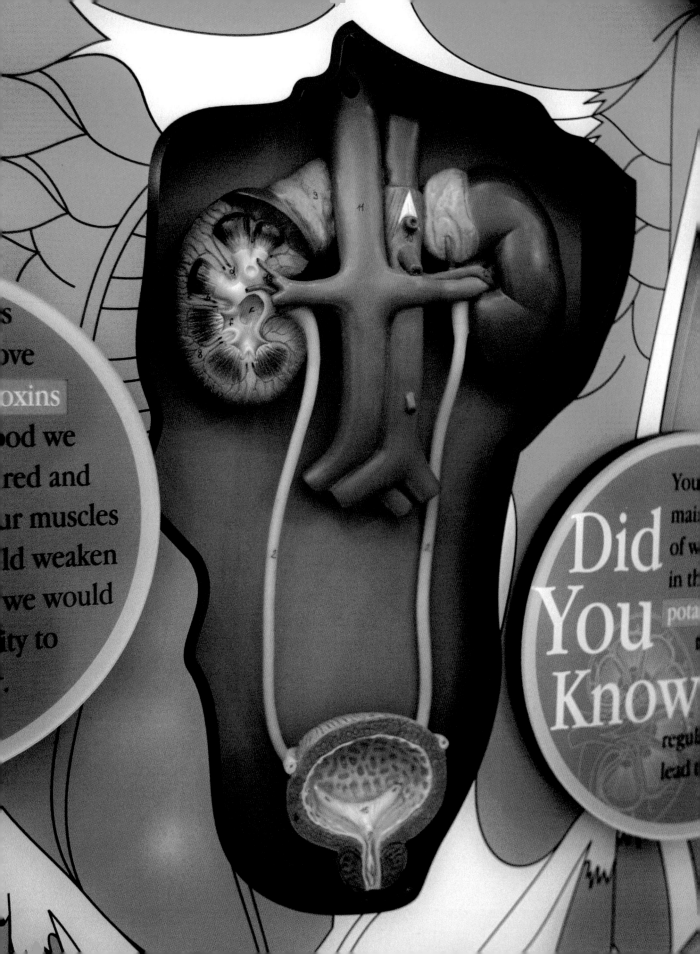

5

Caring for Your Excretory System

Good foods, good hygiene, getting exercise, and avoiding smoking are all great ways to keep your body and all its amazing systems working properly. For the excretory system, there are other tips you can put to use to protect its life-sustaining activities.

FOOD AND DRINK FOR YOUR HEALTH

What does it matter to the urinary system what you eat and drink? Kidneys can usually handle whatever you consume. But there are

Learning about how your body works and how to take care of it is an important step to staying healthy. This display was a part of the National Kidney Foundation's KidneyMobile. The KidneyMobile traveled to different hospitals to help teach people about kidney health and to test for certain kidney illnesses.

Drinking many sugary drinks can cause problems for your excretory system. Too much sugar can also hurt other organs in your body, and cause unhealthy weight gain.

exceptions. One example is drinking a lot of sugary beverages each day. This means that the kidneys are going to be exposed to a lot of sugar each day. Some of it will end up in urine, because it is just too much sugar in the body. Urine that has sugar in it is more likely to nourish bacteria that may be lingering in the urinary tract somewhere. That, in turn, can lead to bacterial infections.

Another problem with a diet that contains a lot of sugar and also a lot of simple carbohydrates (bread, pastries, pasta, pizza crust) is that these foods can make a person overweight. Foods that are high in fats can also cause obesity. Obesity can prevent many different body systems, including the excretory system, from functioning properly.

The best food choices for a healthy excretory system are a combination of vegetables, grains, fruits, and protein-rich foods. It is okay to have sweets

Always read nutrition labels found on the packaging of most food and drinks. The labels can help you maintain a healthy diet and stay away from things that are too high in sugar, salt, or fat.

occasionally, just not several times a day. Fats (butter or margarine, oils, cream, fatty meats) do not have to be avoided altogether, but should be eaten in small quantities. People come in all ages, sizes, and weights and may have different nutritional needs. A nutritionist, doctor, or other healthcare professional can help plan out a healthful diet for a person's specific circumstances and lifestyle.

A well-balanced diet with the right amounts of nutritious food can help you keep your body healthy.

EXERCISE

Everyone talks about how exercise is good for their health. That is true for the excretory system as well. Exercise gets the heart beating powerfully, which, in turn, speeds blood around the body faster. That means blood flows through the kidneys a lot during exercise. Because the kidneys filter waste out of the blood, the kidneys cleanse blood best when they get plenty of it. Additionally, exercise gets everything in the body moving. It helps move toxic substances out of hiding places between cells or even inside them. The toxins are then whisked away through the bloodstream to the kidneys, where the toxins are removed. So, exercise revs up the excretory system's blood-cleansing process.

Exercising can take many forms, from cycling to running or even walking a dog. Experts recommend including some form of healthy physical activity in your daily schedule.

Exercise is also good because it keeps off extra pounds of fat. People who are overweight have a higher chance of getting diabetes, and diabetes is the main reason kidneys get diseased and fail. So maintaining a healthy body weight can help to keep your kidneys healthy.

Exercise can be fun, and it does not need to be hours of grueling push-ups, laps around a track, or weight-lifting. Just half an hour a day of brisk walking, jogging, dancing, swimming, skateboarding, gardening, playing sports, and other physical activities will go a long way toward improving your health.

PREVENTING INFECTION

Almost everybody will have, at one time or another, a urinary tract infection, or UTI. They are the most common urinary tract problem. Millions of people, especially females, get an infection each year. Fortunately, there are easy steps a person can take to prevent them. The main point behind these steps is to keep good personal hygiene, which means to keep your body clean. Tips to prevent UTIS include

- When you bathe, be sure you wash between your legs. Do so gently, with a little soap. Do not rub too hard, but make sure to rinse well. For females especially, soap can be too harsh on the area where the urethra opens.

- After bathing, give the area a chance to dry well before putting on underwear, because bacteria, yeast, or other germs respond to moisture.

- Wear cotton underwear whenever possible, because human-made fabrics, such as nylon and polyester, keep moisture against the body.

- When you have the urge to urinate, do not wait too long. Urine flow washes bacteria out of the urethra.

Using soap when washing your body is essential, but certain chemicals in some soaps can irritate parts of your excretory system. When washing, always use a gentle cleanser, rinse well, and make note of any reactions you may have.

- Drink several glasses of liquids a day, preferably water or low-sugar beverages, to make sure enough plenty of urine is flowing through the system.

- Do not use bubble bath products or fragrances that go in bath water unless they say they are harmless (many product labels warn you not to soak in them because they can irritate the urethra).

- If you are female, after using the toilet, wipe from front to back to prevent bringing bacteria from feces near the urethra.

Drinking the right amount of water can play a part in preventing UTIs and other bladder problems, as well as helping your body stay cool and properly hydrated.

Even those steps may not prevent infection all the time. If signs of infection do start showing up, such as a stinging feeling or pain while urinating, you should schedule a visit with your doctor. They can conduct tests and examinations to see what the problem may be. Depending upon the problem, you might be given antibiotics or other medication to help treat the infection.

CAUTION WITH CHEMICALS

Kidneys filter out all sorts of toxins that might have entered the bloodstream. Because of their job, kidney cells are exposed to higher concentrations of harmful substances than other cells are. The same is true for the bladder since it holds urine for hours at a time. It should be no surprise, then, to learn that kidneys can be permanently harmed by chemicals that are swallowed, inhaled, or rubbed on the skin. Every so often, someone dies from kidney failure after they have been exposed to certain chemicals.

Many of the proven kidney-harming chemicals are not used in households, but are common in factories. As a result, factory workers should always use protective suits, eyewear, and breathing masks.

Harmful chemicals can enter your bloodstream when you inhale them or touch them. Always use gloves, other safety gear, and proper ventilation when handling harsh detergents, cleansers, or other chemicals.

Examples of such chemicals are strong cleansers, petroleum products, liquids used in making plastics, paints, and metal-containing compounds. An example of a dangerous material used outside a factory is ethylene glycol, or antifreeze. This thick, green liquid is used in cars and other vehicles. Unfortunately, pets and even children have died after drinking some of it.

Health experts are coming to suspect that certain everyday chemicals may harm kidneys over time. Some possible examples are nail polish remover, rubbing alcohol, paints, turpentine, certain household cleansers, metals in jewelry (especially body-piercing jewelry), hair dyes, and fumes from carpets and furnishings made of synthetic, or man-made, materials. Some of these things have been shown to harm living cells, or the kidneys of animals, in laboratory studies.

The wisest thing to do is to protect yourself from long-term exposure to too much of these chemicals. If you must use them, use as little as possible. Make sure there is good airflow in the room, or work outdoors. If you can smell the chemical and are using it for more than a few minutes, wear a mask. Wear protective gloves if you are handling a chemical, and goggles if you might splash some. Pay attention to all warnings on a product's label about how to use it safely. You must also be sure to tightly close the lid when you are done, and put the item out of reach of pets or children.

MODERATION WITH MEDICATIONS

Though few people realize it, too much of some of our common medications can harm kidney cells. Most medications are cleared from the bloodstream just like other foreign materials—that is why you need to keep taking daily doses of medication for a while. As a result, kidney cells get exposed to high concentrations of medications. The bladder is exposed, too. But cells of the kidney are more delicate and easily harmed.

Sometimes food supplements and vitamins, minerals, and other natural substances can help keep your body healthy. However, you should never take any supplements without talking to your doctor first.

Still, most of us take medication without it hurting our kidneys. People who are more likely to suffer some kidney damage are those who use high doses of medications, or use them for a long time (several weeks or months), or those whose kidneys already are weakened. That is why it is important to always use a medication as its label explains or as a doctor prescribes. Never use more of a medication than the stated dose. Do not use it longer than the label says you should. And never use medicines that were meant for someone else. Finally, it is a good idea to check with a doctor before taking any medication you have never used—even those on drugstore shelves.

There can be dangers, too, in taking some of the herbal supplements sold as remedies for various health problems. While many are safe, certain ones have sickened and even killed people. An extreme case is what happened with a weight loss remedy made from a plant called Aristolochia fangchi. It turns out that a substance in the plant, aristolochic acid, is very harmful to the excretory system. Seventy people who used the weight loss remedy in Belgium from 1990 to 1992 had to have kidney transplants or dialysis because their kidneys were destroyed. Thirty more people developed

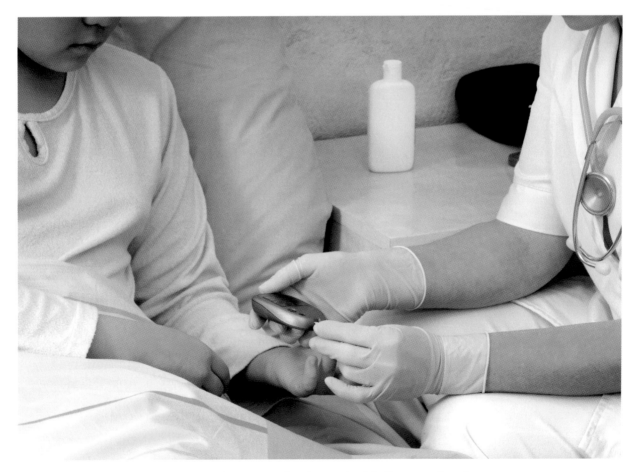

Regular visits to your doctor can help you maintain your health. Every so often they may run tests, such as urine tests or blood sugar tests (shown here), to make sure that your body is working right. Getting checked out can help prevent problems or catch health issues when they are still early enough to treat.

bladder cancer some years later. Hundreds more cases of kidney damage from aristolochic acid have been reported since then. In the United States, it is now illegal for any store to sell a product that contains the acid.

Nowadays, with the Internet, it is easy to look for news and information about a drug or a remedy. So before taking something, it is a good idea to do a search for the name of a drug or herbal product. Look for reports by doctors or health organizations, such as the United States Food and Drug Administration or hospitals, to see if the drugs are harmful—not just to the kidneys, but to other organs as well.

Each of these ideas, from good lifestyle choices to watching out for toxic chemicals, will keep your excretory system healthy. Remember, even though you have two kidneys, you cannot regrow or repair them once they have been damaged. But by taking care of your body, you really can help your kidneys to continue doing their jobs well, with hardly a clue that they are so busy keeping you alive.

bacteria—Single-celled microorganisms that live virtually everywhere on Earth, including on humans and inside them. Some bacteria cause illness and disease.

feces—The waste products made by the digestive system.

germ—A microorganism that causes infections and illnesses. Bacteria and viruses are the most common pathogens.

glomerulus—One of the millions of clusters of tiny blood vessels in the kidney, which leaks fluids that become urine. (The plural of glomerulus is glomeruli.)

hemoglobin—A protein in blood that carries oxygen, and is red in color.

homeostasis—A healthy balance of substances in the body that it needs to survive.

immune cells—The collection of white blood cells in the bloodstream and in immune organs, plus cells scattered throughout the body, which recognize and remove foreign substances.

immune system—The body's team of cells and immune organs (including the spleen, tonsils, thymus, and lymph nodes) that work together to destroy germs and foreign substances.

infection—The presence of harmful bacteria, viruses, parasites, or other microorganisms in the body.

kidney tubules—The millions of tiny tubes in the kidneys that collect fluid as it leaks out of glomeruli (blood vessels). The fluid becomes urine.

pathogen—A microorganism that causes infections and illnesses. Bacteria and viruses are the most common pathogens.

sphincter—A band of muscle that keeps the bladder closed until a person wants to use the toilet.

ureters—The tubes that carry urine from the kidneys to the bladder for storage.

urethra—The tube that brings urine from the bladder to the outside of the body.

urinary tract—The path through which urine travels as it leaves the body.

UTI—Urinary tract infection, which is usually caused by bacteria.

urochrome—A yellowish protein made from worn out hemoglobin, which makes urine yellow.

virus—A microscopic organism that thrives inside the cells of living things. Some viruses are pathogens.

white blood cells (WBCs)—Immune cells found in the blood, but which form in bone marrow and can settle outside the bloodstream in lymph nodes, the spleen, and elsewhere.

Find Out More

Books

Bjorklund, Ruth. *The Circulatory System*. New York: Marshall Cavendish Benchmark, 2008.

Cooper, Sharon Katz. *The Human Body Systems: Maintaining the Body's Functions*. Minneapolis, MN: Compass Point Books, 2007.

Fullick, Ann. *Body Systems and Health*. Chicago: Heinemann Library, 2006.

Gold, Susan Dudley. *The Digestive and Excretory Systems*. Berkeley Heights, NJ: Enslow Publishers, 2004.

Haney, Johannah. *Juvenile Diabetes*. New York: Marshall Cavendish Benchmark, 2005.

Simon, Seymour. *The Human Body*. New York: Harper Collins Children's Books, 2008.

West, Krista. *Urinary Tract Infections*. New York: Rosen Publishing, 2007.

World Book. *The Digestive System and the Urinary System*. Chicago: World Book, 2007.

Websites

Anatomy of the Urinary System
http://www.lpch.org/DiseaseHealthInfo/HealthLibrary/urology/urinaryant.html

Bladder Diseases
http://www.nlm.nih.gov/medlineplus/bladderdiseases.html

Excretory System
http://www.kidsbiology.com/human_biology/excretory-system.php

Kidney Stones
http://www.mayoclinic.com/health/kidney-stones/DS00282

Kidney Stones
http://www.nlm.nih.gov/MEDLINEPLUS/ency/article/000458.htm

Urinary System
http://yucky.discovery.com/flash/body/pg000128.html

Urinary Tract Infections
http://kidshealth.org/teen/infections/common/uti.html

Your Kidneys
http://kidshealth.org/kid/htbw/kidneys.html

Bibliography

American Cancer Society. "Bladder Cancer." http://www.cancer.org/docroot/CRI/CRI_2_1x.asp?dt=44

American Cancer Society. "Kidney Cancer." http://www.cancer.org/docroot/CRI/CRI_2_1x.asp?dt=22

Marieb, Elaine N., *Human Anatomy and Physiology.* 6th ed. Redwood City, CA: Benjamin Cummings, 2003.

MedicineNet.com. "Hemodialysis Treatment for Kidney Failure." http://www.medicinenet.com/hemodialysis/article.htm

MedicineNet.com. "Urinalysis." http://www.medicinenet.com/urinalysis/article.htm

National Diabetes Information Clearinghouse (NDIC). "Diabetes." http://diabetes.niddk.nih.gov/dm/a-z.asp

National Kidney Foundation. "Ten Facts About Diabetes and Chronic Kidney Disease." http://www.kidney.org/news/newsroom/fsitem.cfm?id=3

New York Medical Center. "Cranberry." http://www.med.nyu.edu/patientcare/library/article.html?ChunkIID=21704

Scorecard. "Kidney Toxicants." Scorecard. http://www.scorecard.org/health-effects/explanation.tcl?short_hazard_name=kidn

Springhouse. *Pathophysiology Made Incredibly Easy!* 3rd ed. Philadelphia: Lippincott Williams & Wilkins, 2006.

Index

Page numbers in **boldface** are illustrations.

About the Author

Lorrie Klosterman is a science writer and educator who earned a Bachelor of Science degree from Oregon State University and a Doctoral Degree from the University of California at Berkeley, both in the field of zoology (the study of animal life, including humans). She has taught courses in human health and disease to college and nursing students for several years, and writes about health for a magazine in New York's Hudson Valley. Lorrie Klosterman has also written several health-related books for young adults. Her greatest joy comes from experiencing and learning about the amazing world of animals and plants, and sharing those experiences with others.